Looking at Animals

illustrated by
Wolfgang de Haën
written by
Franz Moisl

Macdonald Educational

Contents

Foreword

This book introduces thirty-eight animals, some of which live close to our human environment and others more distant. They are mainly small and very small animals and they represent the whole diversity of the animal world: birds, reptiles, amphibians, beetles and butterflies. The illustrations and text show where these animals are to be found and describe why certain animals have become very rare: the cutting-down of mixed forests, draining of ponds and the pollution of rivers slowly but surely deprives many animals of their natural habitat.

This book aims to encourage young readers to set out on their own explorations, to observe nature, and to get to know and understand the conditions essential to life for small creatures. It is such a pleasure when, after hours of patient waiting at a pond, you actually discover a dragonfly or kingfisher. Some people may then feel tempted to catch the animal and put it in a cage, so that they can watch it even more closely.

But even if the particular creature is not forced to live in a box with air holes, but is given plenty of water and food, it will never feel at home. Animals need their natural freedom.

The illustrations by Wolfgang de Haën show how animals live in their natural habitat; some of them have already appeared in the magazine 'Parents' and have delighted many children. We hope that this book will do the same.

Franz Moisl
Wolfgang de Haën

Animals in the Garden

This is the sort of garden that animals would like. They do not like cement paths or neat lawns. For garden animals, hedges which can be homes and hiding places and small untidy ponds are much more important. But sadly man uses weedkillers and insecticides which destroy a number of plants and animals on which other animals depend for food. This may make the garden more beautiful for human beings, but for animals it then becomes a more unfriendly place.

It smells with
its feelers

The Cockchafer

About 15 to 20 years ago the cockchafer was very popular with children. They would collect cockchafers in tins, swap their best specimens and even hold cockchafer races. Some years there was a real swarm of cockchafers which delighted the children. But for farmers and gardeners cockchafers are a pest. They eat the leaves of many plants and trees, especially the beech, oak and birch. The larvae of the cockchafers also eat the roots of plants and trees.

What causes cockchafer swarms, and why has the cockchafer now almost disappeared? A cockchafer lives for about four years and two months. It spends four years of that time underground. It only lives four to eight weeks as a fully grown beetle.

The male beetle has a well developed organ in its fan shaped feelers which helps it to pick up the scent of a female beetle. This is called an *olfactory organ*. The male can find a female even when she is several hundred metres away.

In June the female lays her eggs. Over a period of three years they hatch into *larvae*. In the winter of the third year after the eggs were laid the larvae turn into *pupae*. In the following spring the cockchafer emerges and crawls out of the earth. If in one year a lot of beetles develop, then they will also lay a lot of eggs. Even more beetles will then emerge four years later.

When people started to use insecticides the cockchafer was almost exterminated. But you can see many more of them now.

The Hedgehog

A hedgehog rolled up for protection

All land mammals have coats of fur. But the hairs of a hedgehog have hardened and grown into each other to form spikes. It has about 16,000 of these. The spikes of baby hedgehogs are still like soft hair. In a full grown hedgehog they provide a very good defence against its enemies, except its worst enemy, the motor car.

Roughly 300,000 hedgehogs get run over each year in this country. So although you might see one in your garden, you are more likely to find one lying dead on the road. Why is this?

At dusk hedgehogs wander towards asphalt roads, because they store the heat of the sun and stay warmer than grass. This warmth attracts a number of insects which the hedgehog likes to eat. When the hedgehog hears a car approaching, it reacts in the way that it always reacts to danger. It rolls up into a ball for protection. If the first car misses it, it will certainly be killed by the next.

The hedgehog *hibernates* in the winter. This means that it spends most of the time sleeping. It is often curled up fast asleep under a pile of leaves. But a small hedgehog (less than 600 grammes) will not survive the winter. If you find one near the house you should keep it warm. The best thing to do is to keep it in a box in the cellar. Feed it regularly with lean mince-meat, raw or cooked fish, chicken offals, and from time to time with raisins and bits of bananas. It should be given water, not milk, because most hedgehogs get diarrhoea from milk and may die.

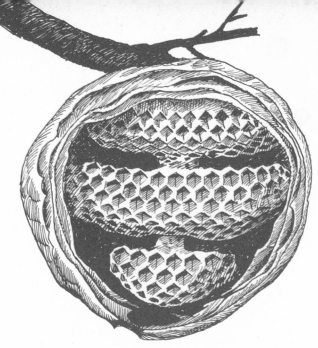

The Wasp

Section of a
common wasp nest

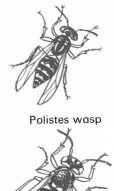

Polistes wasp

Common wasp

Hornet
the largest wasp

Paper was invented in China about 2,000 years ago.
It is made mainly of fine wood scrapings dissolved in
water, spread out and then dried.

Wasps make paper the same way. They use their
strong jaws to scrape off small pieces of wood from old
trees. Then they chew the fine splinters, mixing them
up with their saliva to make a wood pulp. The wasps
stretch out this pulp with their legs and turn it into a
thin, papery substance. They use this for building their
nests.

These grey wasps' nests are usually found in
hay-lofts, barns and attics. Many people are frightened
of removing a wasps' nest. This is quite understandable
because wasps can quickly get angry and sting. In
summer when you eat cake or fruit outside, wasps are
quite likely to fly down onto the food. If you try to
fight them off there is a very good chance that you will
learn how painful a wasp sting can be. It is best to just
keep very still or move quietly out of the way.

But you would be wrong to think that wasps are
simply harmful pests. Like bees, they play an
important part in *pollination*, taking pollen from one
blossom to another. Without pollination most plants
could not produce seeds and there would be no new
plants. It is thanks to wasps that many plants are not
yet extinct.

The Bat

Bats are strange creatures and we do not see them very often. In fact one fifth of all kinds of mammals are bats. They are seen only rarely because most of them live in southern and tropical countries. Only fourteen different species live in the British Isles. They are *nocturnal* creatures, which means that they are active at night. They sleep during the day in caves, lofts, or in holes in the trunks or under the bark of trees. When asleep they wrap themselves into the skin of their wings and hang upside-down. They spend the winter hibernating in the same hanging position.

As bats are nocturnal animals, you might think that they would have large eyes and very good eyesight. But the opposite is true of all common British bats. They have very small eyes and large ears. An Italian scientist called Apallanzani was fascinated by this. He wanted to discover how they could find their way in the dark with such poor eyes. He was the first person to explore this almost 200 years ago. He put wire threads across a room and attached small bells to them. Then he darkened the room, and let some bats fly around. In spite of the total darkness, the bats never touched the wires. But when he also blocked their ears, they often hit the wires.

It was many years later that scientists finally understood how bats managed to guide themselves. One of the sounds that bats make is so high pitched that humans cannot hear it. It is called supersonic sound. They make these sounds whilst flying. The sounds are 'bounced off' solid objects, including insects. Bats have such sensitive ears that when they hear the 'echo' of the sounds that they make, they can tell how far away and what shape the object is.

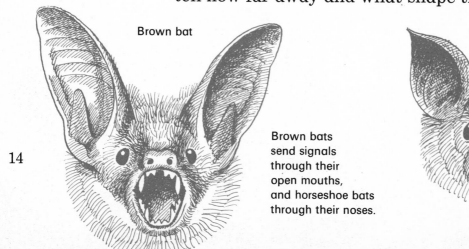

Brown bat

Brown bats send signals through their open mouths, and horseshoe bats through their noses.

Horseshoe bat

14

The Snail

When it is raining you will see a lot of snails out in the countryside. But at other times you do not very often notice these slow-moving creatures that carry their home on their back. Although vegetable gardeners are reminded about snails when they sometimes find that their lettuces have been nibbled! But luckily most land snails usually live off dead and decaying plant matter. Many plants develop hairs or bristles, or contain bitter-tasting parts which protect the plant from being eaten. When the plant is dying, this protection no longer works. Only plants cultivated by man, such as lettuce or grapes, lack this protection. As lettuce contains a lot of calcium, which snails need for building up their shells, it is one of their favourite foods.

The Roman or edible snail has no real tongue, but can still grate up leaves very finely. It does this with the help of a 'grating plate' on the tongue cartilage, which feels and acts like sandpaper.

Roman snails can live for about six years. When they are three years old they are fully developed and ready to reproduce. There is no such thing as a male or female snail. They are *hermaphrodite*. This means that each snail can lay eggs as well as produce sperm. When two snails mate they fertilise each other and then both of them lay their eggs in a hole dug in the ground. The eggs are almost as big as peas, and hatch in three to four weeks. The baby snails are born with a shell the size of a pin-head.

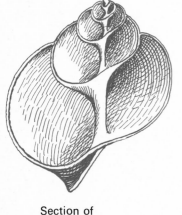

Section of
a snail shell

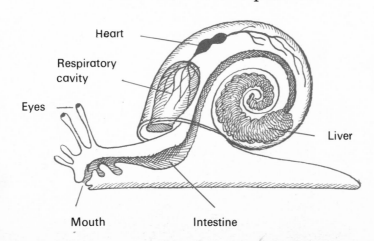

Heart

Respiratory
cavity

Eyes

Liver

Mouth   Intestine

16

The Ladybird

Beetle

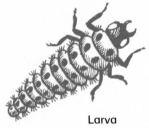

Larva

Pupa

Ladybirds are popular with almost everyone. Even those people who normally dislike insects and go out of their way to kill them seem to have a special affection for the ladybird. They are supposed to bring good luck. Whether they can bring good luck to just one person is doubtful, but they are certainly very useful to the gardener and farmer. Without the ladybird many insects, such as scale insects, mites and especially aphids, would become a real pest.

Ladybirds are a very successful method of pest control. Even the brightly-spotted larva feeds on aphids and can eat about fifty a day. As the female ladybird lays between 500 and 1,000 eggs in her life-time, it is very unlikely that there will ever be an aphid plague. You can use ladybirds in your own garden to keep these pests in check. If you want ladybirds in your garden in spring, you should catch some in October and keep them in a box to hibernate in a frost-free, but cool place.

In winter ladybirds starve if kept in a warm room, unless of course you happen to have pot-plants suffering with green-fly. Ladybirds are not very lively in the winter and normally spend much of the time in a rather sleepy state.

Do not be worried by the yellowy fluid which seeps from the ladybird's six knee joints when they are handled a little roughly. This fluid is a safety device, and has an unpleasantly bitter taste to attackers, but is quite harmless to the human skin.

The Codling Moth

We may often read in fairy stories about a beautiful country where no-one worries about finding something to eat and where everything always tastes delicious! There is one tiny creature which grows up in surroundings which are very close to this idea of a fairy tale land. The larva of the codling moth has no worries about food at the beginning of its life.

The codling moth is a small, rather dull looking moth only a centimetre long. Shortly after the apple trees have blossomed, the female codling moth lays about 80 eggs close to the tiny new apples. The eggs hatch into tiny caterpillars, which eat a long passage through the apple into the core. There they eat first the still unripe pips, and then later they eat the flesh of the apple. In this way the little caterpillar makes itself a cosy home surrounded by delicious juicy apple!

In summer the caterpillar, which by now is big and fat, leaves the almost ripe fruit. It does this by secreting a thread from its abdomen, rather like the spider. This thread hardens in the air. It spends the winter wrapped up in a *cocoon*. The following spring it changes into a *pupa*, called a *chrysalis*, and at the beginning of May the adult moth emerges.

It is not because we envy its pleasant life that we fight and kill the codling moth wherever and whenever we find it. But without the use of insecticides the codling moth would destroy half of the apple harvest every year.

The Earthworm

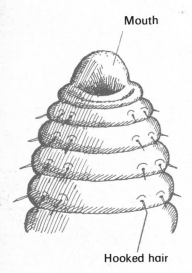

Mouth

Hooked hair

Front end of
the earthworm

If you dig the earth anywhere in your garden, you will almost certainly come across an earthworm. It is not dangerous to pick them up and study them a bit more closely.

The whole of an earthworm's body is divided into equal segments. If you cut an earthworm in half when digging the garden, it does not mean that it will die. The larger part can grow a new head or tail. If you place it on a piece of paper, you will be able to hear small scratching noises. These are caused by the hooked hairs that grow on each segment. The earthworm presses these hairs into the soil when it moves. It can change its shape within seconds. It might be long and thin when you first place it on the paper, and suddenly it is short and fat. By stretching and then contracting its muscles under the skin, it can slowly move through soil. Although you cannot see the earthworm's eyes, it is able to tell the difference between light and dark. Whenever it senses daylight, it will crawl back into the earth as quickly as possible.

It digs a long burrow in the soil and then creates a whole network of tunnels. All this activity churns up the soil, mixing and sifting it. This helps the plants grow and often saves farmers and gardeners from having to dig the earth. The worms feed on decaying plants which they swallow with the soil as they move along in their burrows. Sometimes they even pull bits of plants down from the surface, to eat later.

You are likely to see earthworms after it has rained. Heavy rain sometimes fills the earthworm's burrows with water. It could then suffocate or drown, and in order to breathe it comes up to the surface of the earth.

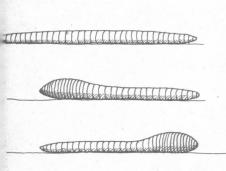

The earthworm moves
its body by stretching
and contracting it.

Field Animals

Nowadays grass is usually cut by a lawn mower not a scythe. These can only work properly on fairly flat ground. That is why farmers make sure that their pastures and fields contain no large stones, bushes or

ditches. Only then can their machines work efficiently and economically. Unfortunately we often forget what happens to the field animals when we clear the land like this. Many animals are killed by the machines, or are left without places to live and breed.

The Hamster

These small, pretty, furry animals store enormous amounts of corn and grain for the winter. The hamster uses its feet to dig a passage straight down into the ground, sometimes as deep as two metres. At the bottom of this passage, it builds its underground dwelling, covering the floor with hay and straw. There is a sloping passage, leading up to the surface, which it uses as an escape route. Many other passages lead to its store-rooms. At the beginning of winter, these store-rooms are already filled with grain. The hamster starts collecting wheat, oats, barley and other grain in the pouches on each side of its face. When these are stuffed full, they look like puffed-out cheeks. It empties its pouches in the store-rooms. In this way the hamster collects up to 20 kilos of corn in its burrow.

Of course this animal is not very popular with farmers. Its other enemies are the buzzard, owl and weasel. Its ability to breed is remarkable. A female hamster can produce a litter of ten young hamsters up to seven times a year. So hamsters could become extremely widespread and do great damage if their natural enemies did not keep down their numbers. Children often keep the small, brownish-golden hamsters in cages as pets. In some countries it has been shown that golden hamsters can be carriers of dangerous diseases such as meningitis.

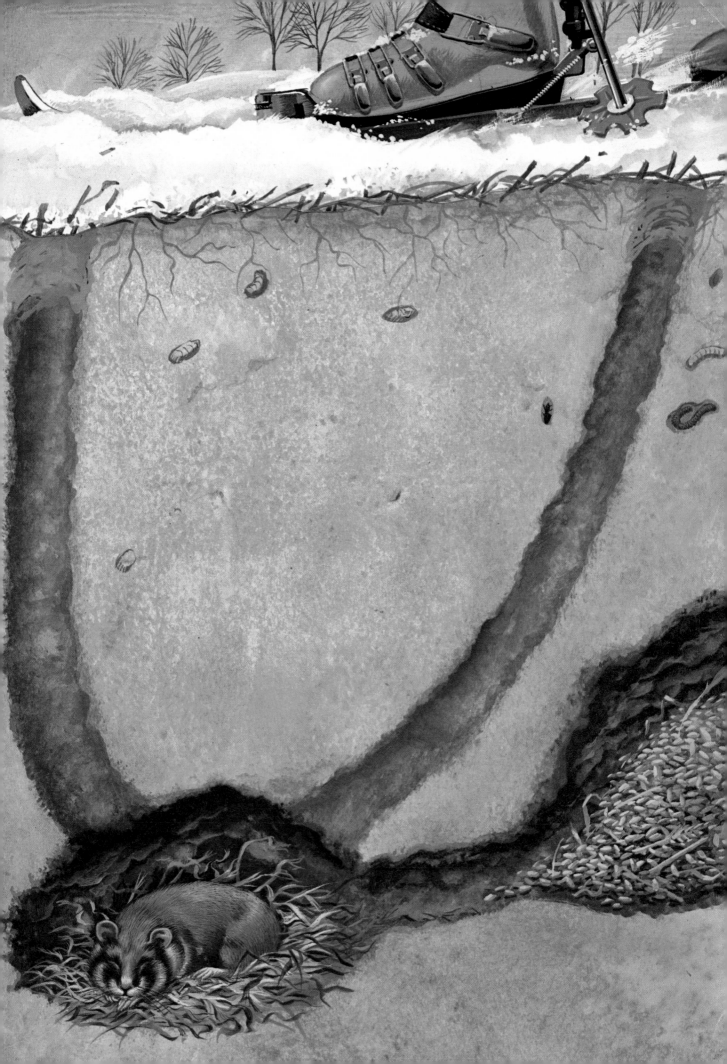

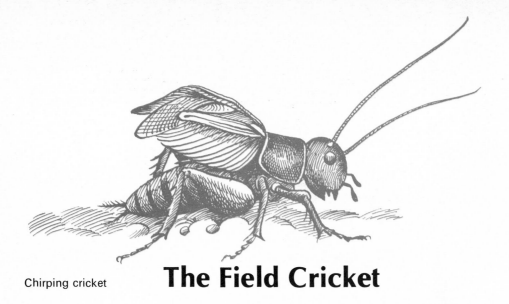

Chirping cricket

The Field Cricket

On sunny days in late spring you will often hear loud chirping sounds out in the fields and meadows. You rarely see the musicians, because as soon as you approach they stop singing. At the slightest vibration of the ground, even a footstep, the cricket disappears into the burrow which it digs for itself. If you study the ground carefully, you will discover the entry hole. If you poke a blade of grass into the opening, the underground inhabitant grips on to it so fiercely that you can pull him out and examine him at close range.

His head is shiny black, quite large and round, with two big eyes and two long, thin feelers which constantly move up and down. The male cricket always lives alone in his burrow and will guard it fiercely against any rival who dares to come near him. When this happens there is usually a violent battle, which ends with the death of one or both of them.

The loud rasping of the male cricket is made rather like the way we make sounds from a violin. The forewings are lifted slightly and rubbed together. The toothed edge of one wing passes over the roughened edge of the other wing, and so makes sounds. The cricket does this to attract the silent females, who have a very sensitive hearing mechanism at the top of their front legs. Even if the song of the male cricket was heard over a telephone by a female cricket held in captivity she would be attracted by the song and try to move towards the receiver.

The Ant Larva

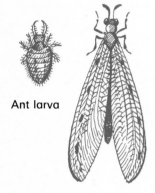

Ant larva

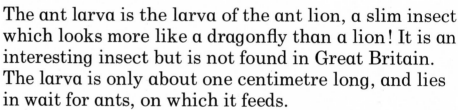

Ant lion (life size)

Claws and head

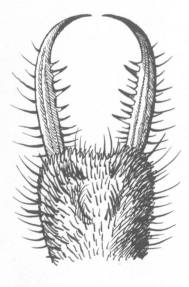

The ant larva is the larva of the ant lion, a slim insect which looks more like a dragonfly than a lion! It is an interesting insect but is not found in Great Britain. The larva is only about one centimetre long, and lies in wait for ants, on which it feeds.

The ant lions lay their eggs in dry, sunny spots in the warm sand. The eggs hatch into long-jawed larva covered in bristles. They have strong jaws, shaped like two powerful claws with which they can grasp other small insects. A narrow tube runs through the inside of these claws. This means that the larva can clasp an ant and suck its insides out at the same time.

In order to prey on as many victims as possible without tiring themselves out, these small hunters have devised a very clever method. They dig a pit, about five centimetres deep, in the soft sand. At the bottom of the pit, well hidden by the sand, they lie in wait for the ants. The ants do not suspect any danger. Once they go over the edge of the pit, they slip on the steep slopes and fall down to the bottom. If the victim tries to scramble up the pit wall again, the ant larva throws sand at the ant and the pit wall and so causes the ant to slide down again.

In early summer the larvae start to turn into pupae. To do this they make a hollow ball out of grains of sand. Some time later the ant lion emerges. You can recognize it by its transparent wings and large round eyes. It is rarely seen during the day, and usually hunts for prey at dusk. It feeds mainly on green-flies.

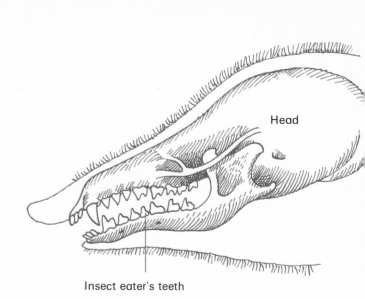

Head

Insect eater's teeth

The Mole

In spring, fields and gardens are often covered with small mounds of earth. After the long winter, the soil of the damp ground is loose and the mole is once again on its search for food.

Although it spends most of its life under ground, the mole does not hibernate like many other animals. So it needs food all year round. In winter the earthworms and grubs, which are its main source of food, burrow down into the lower layers of the soil. The mole then has to dig deeper on its frequent hunting expeditions. For emergency use it stocks up in the autumn and keeps a supply of earthworms in a special larder.

It is not easy to keep earthworms imprisoned in a hole in the ground. As they can eat their way through soil, they could easily escape. But a store of dead worms would be of no use to the mole, because meat goes off very quickly! So the mole solves this problem by squashing the heads of the captured earthworms so that they find it difficult to move. Then whenever it feels hungry the mole has only to get a few worms from its own live stock.

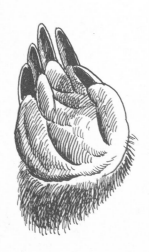

Digging hand

The mole is well-equipped for its life underground. Its front limbs are shovel-shaped. Its fur is soft and shiny and can lie in any direction, so it can quite easily run backwards in the tunnels. Although some gardeners may feel that molehills spoil the look of lawns, the mole is useful to us because it eats up many harmful insects and larvae. It should not be poisoned or trapped.

The Eyed Hawkmoth

How could a harmless moth possibly scare birds?
You might think that that is impossible, but the eyed
hawkmoth, which belongs to the family of hawkmoths,
really does. It is quite common throughout Europe.
But you will see it rarely, as it visits blossoms only at
night. With its proboscis, which is a long hollow
tongue like a suction tube, it draws the sweet-tasting
nectar from the bindweed flower.

During the day the eyed hawkmoth usually stays
completely still on tree trunks, with its wings closed.
Its brownish forewings then look like dead leaves, and
act as a good disguise. They cover the red hind wings,
which have two black and blue eye markings. If a
bird in search of food comes dangerously close to it,
the eyed hawkmoth suddenly brings its forewings
forwards and displays a pair of 'eyes', which stare
threateningly at the enemy. The frightened bird flies
away.

It is practically impossible for any of its enemies to
catch it in flight. With its streamlined body, long
forewings and powerful flight muscles, it is one of the
fastest fliers in the insect world. When it approaches
blossoms, it can hover in the air like a humming bird.
A great deal of heat is created in the eyed hawkmoth's
body because of the quick movement of its wings
during its hovering flight. This is why most
hawkmoths fly only after sunset. The cooler air stops
them from getting too hot.

Chrysalis in the soil

The Great Green Grasshopper

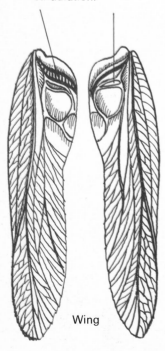

Ear

To sing, the roughened inside edges are rubbed together. This is called stridulation.

Wing

The great green grasshopper belongs to the family of long-horned grasshoppers. They are called long-horned because their feelers—the horns—are usually longer than their bodies. They have long, powerful hind legs, ideal for jumping. Although these insects look harmless enough, you must be careful when picking them up. If the grasshopper feels imprisoned in your hand, it might give your skin a sharp pinch with its strong jaws. Unlike the field cricket, it is not a plant-eater, but feeds on other insects.

The green grasshopper has an amazing jump. It is only between three and four centimetres long, but it can leap straight up into the air as high as one metre, and a couple of metres along the ground. If you compare its size with that of a horse, the horse would have to jump a couple of hundred metres to be able to compete with the green grasshopper. Of course, the grasshopper does use its wings at the same time. You can tell this by the gentle fluttering sound it makes. As they do not like the sun, the best time to watch them is in the early evening or at night.

Towards the end of the summer the female lays eggs in the ground with her *ovipositor*, a curved egg-laying organ which looks like a sting. The eggs hatch as larvae the following spring. Unlike other insects, the larvae already resemble their parents though to start with they do not have wings. Whilst the green grasshopper is still growing, it casts its skin off every so often. This is called *moulting*. After moulting between five and ten times, the grasshoppers are fully developed.

The male can sing like a cricket by rubbing his wings together. The loud rasping sounds attract the silent females, who hear with their forelegs in the same way as crickets.

The Magpie

The magpie has distinctive black and white plumage. All that most people seem to know about it is that it steals sparkling objects and takes them back to its nest. It is often called the thieving magpie. Not so many people know that magpies lead a very dutiful family life.

Male and female work on building the nest together with great patience. It sometimes takes them up to two weeks to build. They nest high up in trees, and protect their homes against birds of prey with thorns and dry sticks.

Unlike many other birds, the male and female magpie stay together for life after they have mated. Although the female hatches the eggs herself, the male looks after her very well. During the entire breeding period, he brings food to the nest and always stays close by. If an enemy approaches, he warns the female with shrill cries so that she has time to escape from the nest.

Once the little birds have hatched, they are fed by both parents. Even after the young ones have left the nest, the family stays together, often until the following winter. During the winter, magpies usually form big sleeping colonies, but in spring most breeding couples reunite. Some magpies migrate in winter, but they return to the same place the following spring.

Magpies cause damage in spring by robbing other birds' nests and killing their fledgelings to feed their own. This is why they are often shot by men.

The Glow-worm

When you are out for a walk on a warm summer
evening, you may well see small, yellow-green
luminous spots flashing across the fields. They
suddenly appear, and then disappear again just as
suddenly. If you stop to watch this closely for a while,
you will realize that the luminous spots flash signals at
regular intervals.

Then you will probably notice luminous spots in the
grass, but these do not move. They are female
glow-worms who cannot fly because they do not have
wings. They climb on to small plants and twist up their
tail segment, which contains the luminous organs. In
this way they reply to the signals of the males flying
around and attract them for mating. You can test this
with a torch. If you flash signals at the same regular
intervals as the female glow-worm, a male will soon
land on the hand holding the torch. You can safely
touch the glow-worm, as the luminous spot does not
burn. The glow is caused by a chemical reaction and is
a 'cold' light. This reaction can also be produced using
a dead, dried-up, glow-worm. All you have to do is
dampen the shrivelled-up luminous organ with water.

Glow-worms hardly feed at all, but their larvae are
very greedy. They even attack snails, which are much
bigger and heavier than themselves. As the larva
cannot eat such a large meal it has to reduce the
snail's flesh into liquid. It does this, by injecting it
with a digestive juice. Then the larva can suck up the
food quite easily.

The Brimstone Butterfly

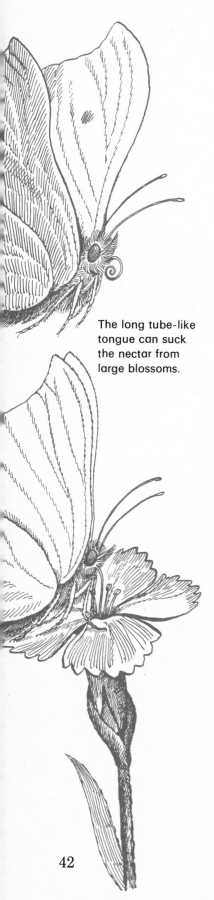

The long tube-like tongue can suck the nectar from large blossoms.

As early as March the brimstone butterfly can be seen fluttering over fields and pastures. After having gone without food for the whole winter, it is searching for the *nectar* of violets and other spring flowers.

It survives the winter in hibernation, hidden in bushes between dry leaves and sticks, or covered by moss. During that time, the butterfly freezes as if in a refrigerator, and its body becomes very delicate and as brittle as glass. In this resting position, the proboscis is neatly coiled up under its head. When the brimstone approaches a flower or when it is sitting on one, it unrolls its tongue to reach into the flower. There it finds nectar, a sweet-tasting liquid which butterflies suck up greedily.

The male brimstone is easily recognizable by its bright yellow wings. The female is a pale greenish-yellow. She lays about 200 eggs, and places them one by one on the buds or the underside of the leaves of the buckthorn or the berry-bearing alder. The green caterpillars hatch in May. They have a white stripe at the side. In June the caterpillar finds a plant stem and attaches itself to it by a silk thread. In this position it waits to turn into a pupa, called a chrysalis. A few weeks later the brimstone butterfly emerges from the chrysalis. It can only fly for a few hours after its transformation, as its wings are still very soft and damp. To expand its wings, the brimstone then pumps blood into them. They dry in the air and slowly harden.

It spends the remaining summer months searching for food before settling down to hibernate in early autumn.

Water Animals

Count the number of different types of animals you can see in this picture. Of course you will never meet all of them at the same time. In fact you might even find it difficult to find just two or three of them. Perhaps you can think of some reason for their disappearance. Many rivers which used to curve their way through the countryside have been artificially straightened. Concrete river beds have been built, and quite often the river now runs through underground pipes. Rubbish tips near rivers and lakes pollute and destroy many animals. With more care much of the damage could have been avoided.

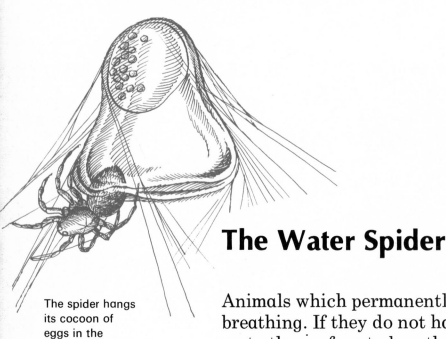

The spider hangs its cocoon of eggs in the diving bell.

The Water Spider

Animals which permanently live in water need gills for breathing. If they do not have gills, they have to come up to the surface to breathe fresh air. Although the water spider has no gills, you have to wait a long time before you see it come up for air.

It can remain under water for hours, because it carries its own supply of air under water. It spins a dense, blanket-like web of silk, which it attaches to water weeds. As soon as its home is completed, it swims to the surface and puts its rear end out of the water. Air is trapped between the spinning organs, the spinnerets, and the body hairs. Beneath the water, the spider empties the bubble of air into the net. It does this until the web is full of air. The web looks like a dome-shaped diving bell. From here it preys on small water animals such as tiny crabs and water insects.

Many threads lead from the bell to the plants surrounding it. These are the water spider's bridges and gangways. It hunts at night, and takes its prey back home into the diving bell to devour it there in peace.

Unlike most other spiders, male and female water spiders live together peacefully. Mating takes place in the female's bell, where she lays between 50 and 100 cocooned eggs. The young spiderlings which emerge from the eggs stay in the diving bell for a few weeks. During that time the female supplies them with air and food.

46

The Fire Salamander

Many of you will only know the fire salamander from pictures, though it is still very common all over Europe. One reason why it is so rarely seen is that it hunts for food only at night. As it does not move very quickly, its prey consists of slower animals such as snails and earthworms. In fact it hardly ever comes out during the day because its skin dries so quickly, especially if the weather is hot. However after there has been some heavy rain it sometimes crawls out of its hiding place.

The fire salamander likes to live in damp, shady woods and near streams. During the day it hides under shrubs and tree trunks, in caves and under stones. Once it has left its hide-out, you can easily spot it because the bright orange-yellow pattern on its black skin gives it away immediately. Unlike other animals which are well camouflaged so that their enemies cannot see them, the fire salamander seems as if it really wants to be found. This becomes less puzzling when we know that a number of glands under its skin discharge fluid which contains acid. The acid causes a painful stinging sensation, especially in the mouth. A bird which has once tried to eat a fire salamander will not try it a second time! The bright yellow spots act as a warning signal: 'Look out—I taste nasty!'

The salamander's moist, cool skin has caused all sorts of strange stories. One of them is that the touch of a fire salamander can put out fires. That is why it is called a fire salamander.

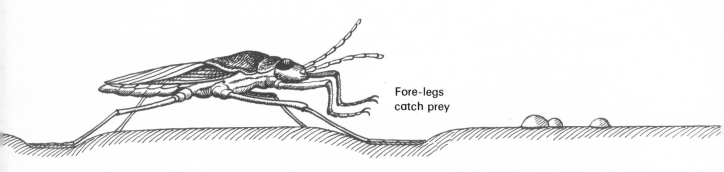

Fore-legs
catch prey

The Pond Skater

These agile little insects skim across the surface of calm ponds, slow-running waters and even puddles. Like skaters, they speed over the water almost without getting their feet wet. If you look at them closely, you will discover that their legs never actually pierce the water. You might think that pond skaters swim in the water—but in fact, they walk across it. Where their feet touch the water they make little dimples. It is as if the water were covered with an invisible layer of skin. Water does in fact have a surface film. The pond skaters can glide elegantly across this.

You can easily see this water skin by doing a simple test at home. Taking great care not to cut yourself, gently place a razor blade flat on the water in a full basin. The blade will remain on the surface, though steel normally sinks. In this case, as with the pond skater, the surface film of the water carries the weight.

The pond skater feeds mainly on small insects which have fallen into the pond, or insect larvae which have come up to the surface for air. It feels the minute waves made by its victim, leaps onto it, seizes it with its short forelegs, and then kills it with its beak-like mouth.

It gets its speed from its long slender middle and hind legs, which balance and steer it across the water. Pond skaters are also good at flying. But you rarely see them in the air. They tend to fly at night when they can see the glistening surface of the water more easily. Even newly formed puddles make a good home for the pond skater.

The Beaver

The beaver can weigh up to 40 kilos, and is the largest
rodent in Europe. It has a flattened tail which it uses
as an oar so that it can swim very fast. It also has
strong front teeth which are always very sharp. A
beaver can even manage to cut down a whole tree. It
does this very cleverly. It gnaws more at the side of the
tree facing the water than at the other. The tree then
always falls into the water, and not on to the land.
But what does the beaver need all these trunks and
branches for?

Beavers are plant-eaters. So long as there is plenty
of juicy green grass, they do not really need to eat
trees. They only feed on bark during the winter.
Usually they need the logs and branches for building
dams to collect water. The entry to a beaver's home or
lodge is always under water. This is a very good
method of protecting the beavers from their enemies.
When a beaver decides to live in a stream which does
not have much water in it, it makes itself a deeper
pond by building a dam across the stream with
tree-trunks, branches and sticks plastered with mud.
The beaver may build a lot of dams making a lot of
ponds with different amounts of water in them. But
the beaver always makes sure that its front door is
under water.

Beaver dam

Beavers used to be found in Great Britain and there
are now plans to introduce families of beavers back
into Britain.

The Dipper

Dippers are shy birds, and are mainly found near the fast running streams of hilly districts in north and west Britain.

Each pair of dippers has its territory stretching over three kilometres. Here the dippers search for small fishes, tadpoles, insects and insect larvae. On the river-bed they walk from stone to stone, wagging their slanting backs rather like wag-tails. A dipper will even wade into deep water with its head well under water. It can remain there for up to 30 seconds.

The dipper turns over pebbles in search of the insect larvae hidden underneath. It uses its wings for balancing, which makes it look as if it were about to fly under the water. It grips on to the stones with its claws so as not to get carried away by the current. When it wants to come up again, it lets go of the stones and floats up to the surface.

In order to avoid water soaking into its plumage, the dipper makes sure that its feathers are always well greased. It gets the oil from its *uropygial* gland, an opening on the back of its body. It presses on the gland with its beak, squeezes some of the oily liquid out, and spreads it evenly over its feathers. The oil prevents water soaking through. With well-preened feathers, it is protected from the wet and cold. It can fly away the moment it steps out of the water, without having to dry its feathers first. And it is always well equipped against icy-cold mountain streams. So long as it keeps this oily protection, a small layer of air always surrounds the feathers. This acts as insulation, even under water.

Young dippers learn to dive and swim before they are taught to fly.

54

The Grass Snake

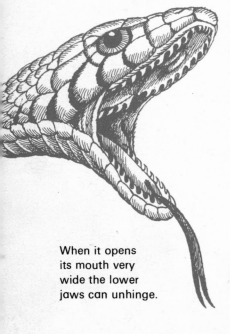

When it opens its mouth very wide the lower jaws can unhinge.

When you are walking beside a lake in summer, you might suddenly hear a rustling sound in the grass or undergrowth. Sometimes you may just see a dark shadow silently disappear into the water. A small head sticks out of the water, and a split tongue flickers in and out from the mouth. It is a grass snake which, disturbed by your footsteps, is making its escape. It is sniffing with its tongue to make sure the coast is clear again.

The grass snake has two openings in its gums, into which it pushes the twin points of its tongue. In order to pick up a smell, it has constantly to put out its tongue. You can see this best when the snake is excited.

The grass snake likes being near water, because there it can easily hunt its favourite prey—frogs. It swallows its victims whole and alive. It is amazing how wide a grass snake can open its mouth. It often takes hours before a large frog reaches the stomach. If the snake is disturbed while devouring its food, it often retches the whole meal up again. Then the lucky, half-swallowed frog can make its escape unharmed.

In summer the grass snake lays between twenty and thirty eggs, which are surrounded not by a shell, but a fine skin. It usually chooses a dung or compost heap to lay its eggs, because the warmth there helps the eggs to hatch more quickly.

Unlike adders, grass snakes are not poisonous and can not hurt you. So never kill one just because you are frightened of snakes. Just leave it in peace.

The skeleton

The Kingfisher

The kingfisher can be found almost everywhere in Europe, except in Northern countries where there is a lot of snow and ice. This strikingly colourful bird, with its emerald green plumage, comes originally from the tropical countries. And that is where the majority of kingfishers still live.

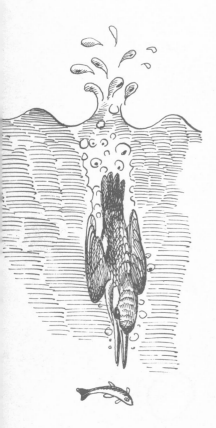

Kingfishers have a long pointed beak, like that of the woodpecker. They use it for catching fish, and for building burrows in the banks of rivers and lakes. They often wait for hours, perched on a twig overlooking the water. Once the kingfisher has seen a small fish, it plunges headlong under the water and grabs the fish with its dagger-like beak. In a flash it turns around under water, swims up to the surface and pushes itself off again with its wings. The whole incident takes less than a second. Although the kingfisher only catches small or injured fish, it has been hunted ruthlessly by fish-breeders.

Kingfishers only nest along clean, fish-carrying waters, and as most of our lakes and streams are becoming more and more polluted, they have been driven away from many areas. The young kingfishers are always in danger. Rats and weasels can force their way into the nest through the one metre long burrows in the river banks and kill the young. Some young kingfishers drown when they first hunt for fish.

The Emperor Dragonfly

Between the months of June and August you can see the blue and black emperor dragonfly near lakes and ponds. This must be one of the most beautiful insects. They dart past you, or hover in mid-air. Sometimes they even fly backwards. Unlike other insects, they can move each of their four wings independently, or two at the same time in opposite directions. By doing this, the dragonfly can hover in the air. When using all four wings together, it can reach a top speed of up to 90 k.p.h.

Many people are frightened of these beautiful insects, and run away the moment they catch sight of a dragonfly. This is difficult to understand. Perhaps it is because of their enormous eyes and their powerful claspers. Dragonflies are certainly very dangerous to other insects, but not to us. They catch their victims whilst flying very fast and devour them while still in the air. All the time their huge eyes are looking around for more prey.

The nymph or larva of the dragonfly is also a great hunter. It has a large lower lip armed with a pair of pincers. This is called a mask. The nymph lives in the water, and usually lies in wait for its prey, hidden in the mud. As soon as a tadpole or small fish approaches, it shoots out its mask at the passing victim and grasps it with the pincers.

The nymph breathes through gills in its intestines. So water has to pass in and out of the intestine all the time. If in danger, the nymph immediately presses the water out. This jets it away from the danger area within seconds.

The larva's mask

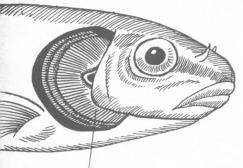

Behind the gill-covers
are the gills
with which the
fish breathes.

The Minnow

The minnow is a small, freshwater fish, more
commonly known to children as 'the tiddler'. It is
found in lakes, rivers and streams all over Britain and
the rest of Europe. Because it is so small, it is often at
risk from larger fish. It does, however, have a very
useful warning system.

Not all fish are silent. There are some which use
their air bladder to make croaking or squeaking
noises. But tests have shown that minnows can warn
their shoal of approaching dangers, such as hungry
fish, without making a sound.

For example when a pike attacks a shoal and eats
one of the minnows, the rest of the shoal become
extremely agitated, even though they might not have
seen the attack taking place. This agitation begins as
soon as the skin of one of the minnows has been
punctured. These small fish have glands under the skin
which contain an alarm substance. Once the skin has
been pierced the substance leaks into the water. The
other minnows pick up the scent, recognise danger,
and scatter in all directions to avoid the enemy.

Minnows can also change the colour of their skins,
disguising themselves according to their surroundings.
Against a pale background their skin seems pale, and
against black it changes to a darker colour within
minutes. The minnows' skin contains a pigment which
enables them to do this quite simply.

The Toad

Toads have always been disliked and many people shudder at the sight of them. Why is this? Part of the reason may be the look of a toad's skin. It is covered in warts. These warts are in fact a collection of poison glands. When an enemy approaches, the toad first tries to escape. If the enemy catches up with it, the glands send out a slimy substance which has an unpleasant smell. This liquid irritates the sensitive lining of the attacker's nose and mouth. It does not harm people.

In the Middle Ages some people thought that every toad had a precious stone in its head—the toadstone. This stone was thought to have magic powers. Witches were meant to know all the strange ways of finding and using the toadstone to help with their magic. This may be another reason why many people do not like toads.

This picture shows a changeable toad now very rarely found in Central Europe. It is really quite a beautiful toad. Even the male's voice sounds quite pleasant! It is more like the whistle of a canary, than a frog's croak. As the changeable toad, like all other toads, feeds mainly on harmful insects, it is an extremely useful animal. You should always leave toads in peace and not drive them away or kill them.

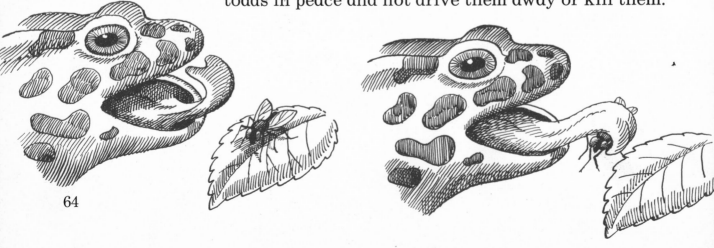

The Black-headed Gull

The black headed gull is found all over Europe, but not always at the seaside. It is usually found by still or slow-running inland waters. It is easily recognizable by the red beak, bright red legs and during breeding time in summer, its very dark brown, nearly black head. In winter the head is white.

In winter, whole flocks of black headed gulls descend on large cities to find food. They will readily accept bread that is offered to them, though normally they prefer to feed on fish, insects and worms.

Gulls are such good fliers that if you throw up a piece of bread, they can usually catch it in mid-air. If they miss and it falls into the water, they will dart after it. Just before they reach the surface they will brake, seize the bread, and then fly on without really touching the water at all. Even if the bread has sunk, the gull will not give up immediately. It lands on the water or swims to the spot, and dives after the food using its webbed feet.

This gull's nest is an untidy heap of decaying water-plants and reeds. The female lays three greenish-blue eggs, which are incubated by both birds. This means that they take it in turns to sit on the eggs and keep them warm. After about 20 days the little gulls hatch. They are continually hungry and are always screaming for food. The parent gulls are then constantly out searching for snails, worms and grubs.

Forest Animals

The woodland should be a place of peace and rest for people. But if you go out for a walk in the woods at the week-end near any large town, you will find that this is not true at all. Some people picnic and simply throw empty bottles and plastic bags into the bracken. Others make such a lot of noise driving their motorcycles along the narrow paths or playing radios very loudly that it is not surprising that animals avoid these places completely. Another reason is that mixed forests are becoming scarce now. These are generally being replaced by pine-woods where trees grow so densely that there is not enough light on the ground for grasses, mosses and bracken. So there are fewer homes for animals.

The Wood Ant

The wood or red ant's nest is easily recognized by its size, up to two metres high, and because of the way that it is made of layers and layers of pine-needles, leaves and earth stacked up. On sunny days huge numbers of ants are seen crawling outside the nest. Considering the vast number of ants living in such a nest, anything up to 100,000, it is difficult to imagine any sort of organized life inside it. Yet life inside is very well organized indeed.

In the wood ant's nest there are three kinds of inhabitant. First of all, there is the queen. She is the only one in the whole colony who can lay eggs. She is looked after by the workers, the sterile females. Those that cannot lay eggs. They take on the nest-building, food-gathering, nursing of the young ants and the defence of the colony. Males are only found in the nest just before the mating flight. Their job is simply to fertilize the future queen during this flight. As they cannot feed themselves, the males then soon starve. During the mating flight the queen stores the males' sperm in a bag in her body to keep it fresh and she can then do without a male for as long as 12 years.

Winged female

Winged male

Worker

An ant returns home and feeds another ant in the nest.

Ants like all sweet-tasting food. For this reason they keep their own herds of aphids. Aphids suck the sap from plants with their proboscis. Some of this sap is excreted as sugar. The ants are very fond of this sweet substance.

If each ant ate only one other insect per day, then a whole colony would destroy about 100,000 harmful insects every day. This is the reason why the wood ant is now protected. You should therefore never kill ants, or destroy their nests.

The young cuckoo throws everything out of the nest.

The Cuckoo

At the edge of heaths, woods and moorlands you can begin to hear the cuckoo's call all day long in late spring. With this call the male signals that it has returned from Africa and is occupying its rightful territory again. Any strange male cuckoo that dares to trespass is looking for trouble.

Almost everyone knows the cuckoo's call, but few have actually ever seen this bird, which is about the size of a pigeon. The cuckoo is very shy, and will immediately withdraw into the wood if approached.

Most birds build nests so that they can lay their eggs there and bring up their young. If anyone ever tells you that he has seen a cuckoo's nest, you will know that it is not true. The cuckoo does without a nest of its own because it has its eggs hatched out by other birds. In order to deceive the future foster parents, the female cuckoo works out a very clever plan. At a suitable moment she lays an egg and carries it in her beak to a nest which just happens to be unguarded. Usually she simply swaps it for one of the eggs already in the nest. Although the cuckoo is usually much larger than the chosen foster parents, its eggs are the same size. They are often the same colour too.

The young cuckoo hatches after only twelve days. This is between one and three days earlier than its step brothers and sisters. On the very first day after hatching, the young cuckoo tries to push anything touching it out of the nest. In this way it forces the other eggs or fledglings from the nest. The foster parents are apparently not worried by this and they carry on feeding the young cuckoo.

The Stag Beetle

The largest beetle found in this country has unfortunately become rather rare. In Central Europe it is now protected so that it does not disappear altogether. One reason why there are no longer so many stag beetles is that they usually live in woods where oak-trees grow. Wood has become very valuable and so fast growing trees such as pines are more often planted nowadays. Oaks grow very slowly and are therefore rarely used for replanting.

Female stag beetles, which grow to only half the size of the male, lay their eggs in rotting oak-tree stumps. Once the larvae have hatched, they feed on the rotting oak wood. Wood is in fact indigestible, and not a suitable food for insects. It is the minute fungi causing the rotting of the wood which the stag beetle larvae actually live on. It takes between three to five years for the larvae to become fully-sized stag beetles.

Male stag-beetles have very large upper jaws, which look like antlers. That is why we call them stag beetles. Although these jaws look very dangerous, the stag beetle itself is quite a peaceful animal. It lives on plant matter only. The sweet sap which comes from oak trees when the bark is cut, is a real delicacy for the stag beetle. Sometimes two males may actually fight over some tasty morsel. It is then that they use their antlers. They grab each other with their big claws, and try to push each other off the tree. But even if the weaker of the two falls off, it will not be injured, because it is protected by a strong wing case.

The Wood Mouse

A nut chewed
by the mouse.

How can an animal which is hardly ever seen be the most common mammal in Europe? It is certainly much easier to get a look at many other mammals.

The wood mouse is very timid and moves extremely fast. It usually stays in its nest in the ground or under the roots of trees during the day. That is why it is so rarely spotted. Whenever it does cross your path, it rushes past so quickly that you will scarcely be able to recognize it.

You might well have caught a glimpse of the wood mouse without knowing it. In winter it often moves into houses and flats, and is easily mistaken for the house mouse. It is much prettier than the house mouse. Its best features are unusually large eyes and ears, as well as a yellow stripe in its fur, running from the throat to the chest.

Like the house mouse, the wood mouse is an omnivorous animal. This means it will eat almost anything. In fact it lives mainly on nuts, corn, acorns or beechnuts, but it also eats insects and worms. For the winter it hides a stock of acorns and nuts, because it does not hibernate and so needs food during the cold season. About three times a year the wood mouse produces a litter of between six and eight young. At birth they are blind and naked. After a week their eyes open and their hair begins to grow. If the mother falls victim to a tawny owl on one of its nightly searches for food, her young will die as well. This is because they are suckled by the mother for up to six weeks and so without her they starve.

The Sparrowhawk

The sparrowhawk is found throughout Britain and
Ireland. Its main prey is small birds and it causes them
a lot of trouble. The use of pesticide on seed crops
meant that sparrowhawks became almost extinct in
1963. Many of them died because they had eaten
poisoned seed-eating birds.

The sparrowhawk lives in small coniferous forests,
and can sometimes be seen flitting through the
branches. It flies around the edge of the wood on the
look-out for suitable prey. Once it has discovered a
group of small birds such as sparrows, it will dart
down. Terrified, the birds scatter apart trying to
escape, but for one of them it is usually too late.
Diving down and turning sharply in flight, the
sparrowhawk grabs its victim with its strong talons
and kills it instantly. The hawk then finds a quiet spot
to pluck its prey. All that remains of its meal are the
large bones which the sparrowhawk cannot swallow.

While the cocks are content with sparrows and
songbirds the female, which is considerably larger, will
also kill pigeons, jays and in winter even partridges.

Sparrowhawks usually build their nests in dense
thickets out of twigs and small branches. The hen only
starts breeding at the beginning of summer, when
other young birds have already hatched. By that time
a rich choice of young birds provide plenty of food.

Both parents are involved in bringing up their
young. The male does the hunting, and the female
feeds the little ones. The prey has to be picked over
very carefully for the chicks to be able to swallow it.
Only the hen knows how to do this. If she dies the
chicks die as well, even though the cock will still bring
food to the nest.

The Tree Frog

Unlike the toads and common frogs disliked by most people, the European tree frog is one of the more popular amphibians. Tree frogs are not found in Britain and even on the Continent they are in danger of being exterminated. The biggest threat to their survival does not come from the gourmets, the people who enjoy a tasty frog's leg, but from the changing environment.

Frogs not only breathe through the skin, they also 'drink' through their skin. If the bushes and trees of their living area are sprayed with pesticides, the frogs soak up this poison through their body. The tadpoles too, which hatch from the frog-spawn and can only live in water, are extremely sensitive to environmental poisons polluting the water. Rubbish dumped near a stream or pond can destroy all the frog-spawn. When ponds and ditches are drained, the frogs are deprived of their natural environment.

Frogs travel many miles every year to reach familiar spawning grounds. More and more often they are forced to cross busy roads and even motorways. With the heavy traffic on such roads, only a small number of frogs get across safely.

Quite a few people like to catch frogs and then keep them in a jam jar. This is very cruel. It is really much more enjoyable to observe a tree frog or any other frog in its natural environment, instead of keeping these useful insect-eaters imprisoned.

The males croak loudly by swelling their throats.

80

The Spotted Woodpecker

The spotted woodpecker's natural home is the forest. With a bit of luck you can also come across it in parks and some gardens. Although you might not spot it straight away, you can hear it drumming from a long way away. In the past people believed that this loud noise was made to startle the insects under the bark so that the woodpecker could eat them when they came up to the surface. We now know that the woodpecker's drum is a call note by which the male hopes to attract the female.

When it is searching for food it does something quite different. It runs up and down the tree trunk, even head-first towards the ground if necessary and listens for the gnawing sounds of tree-insects living under the bark. Once it has discovered a weevil, bark-beetle or one of their larvae, it winkles them out of grooves and cracks in the bark with its long, thin and sticky tongue. The spotted woodpecker is a useful creature because it helps to keep down wood-pests in woods and forests.

The tongue can go round the inside of the head once and can stretch to four times the length of the beak.

In winter the spotted woodpecker changes to a vegetarian diet, and no longer feeds on insects. It searches for fir and pine seeds or hazelnuts. It skilfully squeezes the nuts into cracks in the bark, and hammers their shells open with its beak.

Woodpeckers build their nests in rotten tree-trunks. When they have done this, the trees look as if they have been carved with a chisel. The spotted woodpecker is a very good carpenter!

The Long-eared Owl

Young owls.

It is practically impossible to spot a nocturnal hunter like the long-eared owl. During the day it usually sits still against the trunk of a tree, well hidden by branches and leaves. Long-eared owls live in coniferous woods, but they can also be found in parks and wooded cemeteries. They are now rare in Britain.

If you do ever see a long-eared owl, you will probably think that it looks rather strange. Its odd appearance is due to its large eyes, surrounded by a ruff of feathers, called the facial disc, and the two ear tufts on its head. The two tufts are feathered ear-flaps which can be held erect. If disturbed, the long-eared owl pricks up its ear tufts in order to scare the intruder.

Long-eared owls feed mainly on field mice and voles, and are extremely useful to us. They rarely kill young birds, and when they do the young birds are usually either weak or injured. All the same, small birds, crows and even larger birds will burst into shrieks of alarm when a long-eared owl approaches.

When it hunts at night, you can hear its ghostly hooting sounds in the forest. Its large eyes help it to spot its prey clearly even in the dead of night, and its velvety soft feathers enable it to swoop down on its unsuspecting victim without making a sound. First it tries to swallow the prey whole. If it does not succeed it breaks up the fur and bones with its beak and feet, and then devours the individual pieces. As hair, feathers and bones are indigestible, they are regurgitated some time later. These tell-tale remains, called pellets, are seen more often than the owl itself.

The Long-tailed Tit

You can see immediately how the long-tailed tit's name came about. Its tail is much larger than its body. The best times to watch it are during spring and autumn, when it roams woodlands and parks in search of food. Long-tailed tits are very useful animals because their diet consists of insects and insect larvae.

The male and female build their nest together. They sometimes choose forked branches, but best of all they like thorn-bushes, hedges or dense blackberry bramble. The male fetches the building material continually carrying mosses, lichens and blades of grass to its skilful partner. Small pieces of bark or empty cocoons are often used in building the nest. The long-tailed tit artistically spins the building materials into a domed nest with an opening at the side. The outer walls are covered with the same lichens as those growing on the nesting tree. When finished it is very difficult to find the beautifully hidden nest.

Once the hard work of building the actual structure has been finished the tit can concentrate on the interior of the nest. It is lined and padded with hair, feathers and even wool. Long tailed tits' nests have been found containing more than 1,000 feathers. This soft lining provides warmth for the eggs and the young. The nest takes as long as three weeks to build, and then the female lays about a dozen eggs inside it. Very shortly after the eggs have been hatched, the nest becomes too small for the large family. The chicks push each other for the best place and so cracks and holes begin to appear in the nest. For comfort the young birds poke their tails through the cracks. Then the nest looks like a huge shuttlecock!

The Crossbill

The crossbill is not much bigger than a sparrow, and usually lives in *coniferous* forests. Its most outstanding feature is its beak, which is shaped rather like a parrot's bill but with crossed tips. The crossbill also moves like a parrot. When climbing up a tree, it holds on to the branches with its bill and then pulls itself up.

Fir and pine seeds are the crossbill's favourite food. It requires great skill and strength to crack the cones and extract the hidden seeds. The crossed bill is especially suited for this task. The crossbill manages to press its bill under the scales. It then prises them off and licks out the seeds which are hidden underneath. You will see a lot of crossbills when there is a rich cone harvest. They fly from one pine plantation to another in large flocks, in search of the best feeding sites.

As pine cones only ripen in autumn and remain on the tree for the whole of the winter, the crossbill can find plenty of food during the cold season. That is why it breeds not only in summer, but even in the middle of winter.

When the young crossbills hatch they have straight bills. The bill-tips start to cross three weeks later. At first the parents feed the young crossbills with seeds. Later they take the whole cones to the nest and teach the young to extract the seeds for themselves. Crossbills are friendly birds and become tame very quickly in captivity. But it would be very cruel to keep a wild bird like the crossbill in a cage.

A young crossbill

Index

Glossary

Amphibian: A creature that can live on land and in water.

Cocoon: The silken covering that many caterpillars spin around themselves before turning into pupae. The water spider wraps its eggs in a cocoon.

Chrysalis: A hard cased pupa.

Coniferous trees: Cone bearing trees, usually evergreen.

Deciduous trees: Trees that lose their leaves annually.

Hermaphrodite: A creature that is both male and female at the same time.

Hibernate: To spend the winter in a sleepy state.

Larva: The second stage in an insect's development which takes place between the time it leaves the egg and the time it becomes a pupa.

Mask: **(of the dragonfly larva):** The enlarged lower lip which is armed with a pair of hooks.

Moult: To cast off skin, fur or feathers. A snake **sloughs** its skin.

Nectar: A sweet tasting liquid in flowers collected by bees to make honey.

Nocturnal: This describes any animal which is active only at night.

Nymph: The state before the dragonfly larva becomes a flying insect.

Olfactory organ: The smelling organ.

Ovipositor: A curved egg-laying organ. It looks like a sting.

Pollen: A powdery substance produced by flowers. Bees are one of the insects that collect the pollen for food. As they fly from flower to flower, they accidentally leave grains of pollen from one flower in a different flower. This fertilises the flowers.

Pollution: The spoiling of the environment by poisons, industrial waste, spilled oil and rubbish.

Pupa: The third stage in an insect's development. It is a resting stage before the whole adult insect emerges.

Uropygial gland: The gland which produces an oily water-resistant liquid. The dipper spreads this liquid on its wings to protect its feathers when diving.

First published 1978 by Macdonald Educational Limited
Holywell House
Worship Street
London EC2A 2EN
This licensed edition © Macdonald Educational Limited 1978
ISBN 0 356 06139 6

Originally published 1977 by
Otto Maier Verlag Ravensburg
as Wir entdecken Tiere by
Wolfgang de Haën and Franz Moisl
All illustrations © Otto Maier Verlag Ravensburg
This authorised translation from the German by
Neil and Roswitha Morris
Cover illustration by Tony Payne
Cover illustration © Macdonald Educational Limited 1978

Printed in Italy by New Interlitho SpA